MACDONALD STARTERS

Homes

Macdonald/London

About Macdonald Starters

Macdonald Starters are vocabulary controlled information books for young children. More than ninety per cent of the words in the text will be in the reading vocabulary of the vast majority of young readers. Word and sentence length have also been carefully controlled.

Key new words associated with the topic of each book are repeated with picture explanations in the Starters dictionary at the end. The dictionary can also be used as an index for teaching children to look things up.

Teachers and experts have been consulted on the content and accuracy of the books.

Illustrated by: Christine Sharr

Editors: Peter Usborne, Su Swallow

Reading consultant: Donald Moyle, author of *The Teaching of Reading* and senior lecturer in education at Edge Hill College of Education

Chairman, teacher advisory panel: F. F. Blackwell, general inspector for schools, London Borough of Croydon, with responsibility for primary education

Teacher panel: Elizabeth Wray, Loveday Harmer, Lynda Snowdon, Joy West

First published 1971 by Macdonald and Company (Publishers) Limited
St Giles House
49-50 Poland Street
London W1

This is our home.
We live at home
with Mummy and Daddy.

1

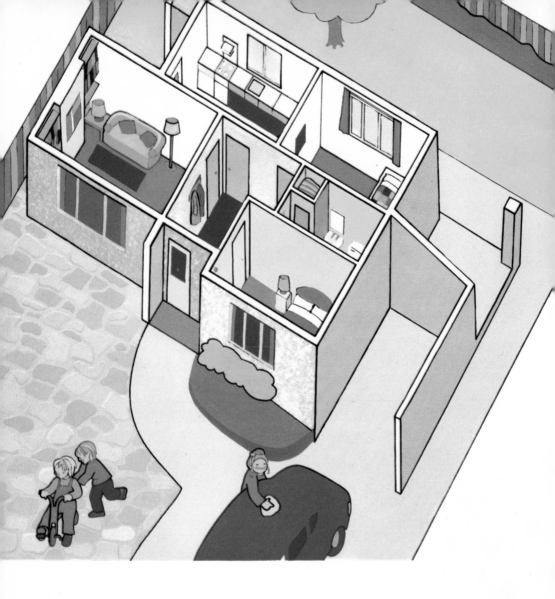

There are five rooms in our home.
Our home is a bungalow.
It has no upstairs.

2

This is our room.
It has a red carpet.
We have funny pictures on the wall.

This is the kitchen.
Mummy cooks in the kitchen.
She can see out of the window.
4

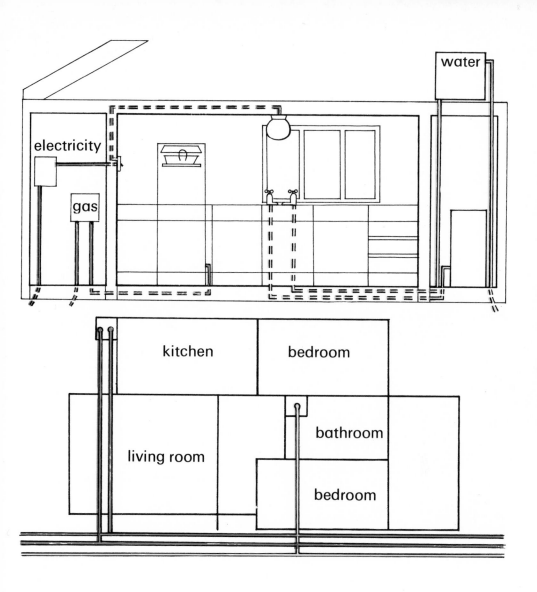

Our kitchen has
electricity, gas and water.

Long ago people made homes in caves.
They drew pictures on the wall.
They cooked with fire.

6

Some people lived in pile dwellings.
The houses stood in water
on long poles called piles.
There are still some pile dwellings today.

Some people learnt to build.
These people found big stones.
They built stone huts.

8

In cold lands there is snow.
People build huts of snow.
The huts are called igloos.
It is warm inside an igloo.

Here there are lots of trees.
Houses are made of wood.
Thick snow slips off the steep roof.

These houses are made of mud.
People make mud bricks.
The sun bakes the mud hard.

11

These houses are made of bricks too.
The bricks are small and red.
The bricks are made of baked clay.

Gypsies like to move their homes.
Gypsies live in caravans.

These people must move their homes.
They take their animals
to find fresh grass.
They live in tents.
14

Other people live in tents too.
People take tents on holiday.

Kings lived in palaces.
Palaces were very big homes.
Kings were very rich.

16

This is a castle.
Castles were very strong homes.
They were safe in war.

Most homes are near other homes.
These are in a village.
The people can help each other.
They sell things to each other.

18

Lots of homes make a town.
Here is a town of long ago.

19

More and more people live in towns.
They cannot all have houses.
There is no room.
People live in blocks of flats.

20

Many people live near towns.
They work in the town.
They go to work every day.
The trains get too full.

See for yourself

Can you draw a plan of your home?
Write in the names of the rooms.
22

Starter's **Homes** words

bungalow
(page 2)

window
(page 4)

carpet
(page 3)

cave
(page 6)

picture
(page 3)
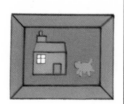

fire
(page 6)

kitchen
(page 4)
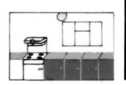

piles
(page 7)

23

roof
(page 7)

caravan
(page 13)

stones
(page 8)

tent
(page 14)

igloo
(page 9)

palace
(page 16)

brick
(page 11)

castle
(page 17)

gypsy
(page 13)

flats
(page 20)
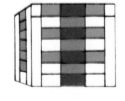